NATIVE NATIONS OF THE
SOUTHEAST

BY THERESE NABER

Published by The Child's World®
1980 Lookout Drive • Mankato, MN 56003-1705
800-599-READ • www.childsworld.com

Acknowledgments
The Child's World®: Mary Berendes, Publishing Director
Red Line Editorial: Editorial direction and production
The Design Lab: Design
Content Consultant: Dr. Lavonna Lovern, Native American
Studies, Valdosta State University

Photographs ©: Eve Edelheit/The Tampa Bay Times/AP
Images, cover, 2; Shutterstock Images, 1, 28; Red Earth
Festival CC 2.0, 3 (top), 14; Gerald Herbert/AP Images,
3 (middle top), 34, 36–37; Jeffrey M. Frank/Shutterstock
Images, 3 (middle bottom), 18; Melissa Cherry/The Herald/
AP Images, 3 (bottom), 30; iStockphoto, 5, 39; Jerry Willis/
Muskogee Daily Phoenix/AP Images, 6; Carol M. Highsmith/
Library of Congress, 7; National Geographic Creative/
Corbis, 8; Miguel Juarez Lugo/ZumaPress/Corbis, 10; Sue
Ogrocki/AP Images, 11, 15; Department of Transportation/
U.S. National Archives and Records Administration, 12; Danzil
Raines CC 2.0, 16; Smithsonian Institution, 19; Elliott Minor/
AP Images, 20; Ed Kashi/VII/Corbis, 22; Natalie Maynor
CC 2.0, 23; Brad Holt CC 2.0, 24; Lou Krasky/AP Images,
26; Library of Congress, 27; iStock/Thinkstock, 29; Patrick
Semansky/AP Images, 32

ISBN: 9781634070355
LCCN: 2014959806
Printed in the United States of America
Mankato, MN
July, 2015
PA02269

ABOUT THE AUTHOR

Therese Naber is a writer who lives in Minnesota. She has coauthored more than ten textbooks and workbooks for students and teachers of English as a second language. She has also written many tests and online activities for language learning.

Seminole Nation members participate in a procession.

TABLE OF CONTENTS

ARCTIC

OCEAN

GREENLAND

Gulf of
Alaska

Hudson
Bay

CANADA

PACIFIC

OCEAN

ATLANTIC

OCEAN

UNITED STATES

KEY

Southeast
Native Nations

N
W   E
S

MEXICO

Gulf of
Mexico

CHAPTER ONE

SOUTHEAST NATIVE NATIONS

The southeast region of the United States has warm weather and lush plant life. The area covers approximately 400,000 square miles (1 million sq km). The Appalachian Mountains lie in parts of present-day Tennessee, Georgia, and the western Carolinas.

The swamps of southern Florida are one of many environments in the southeast United States.

Actors tell a Cherokee legend at the Cherokee Heritage Center in Oklahoma.

East of the mountains is the Piedmont Plateau. This area has rolling hills, rivers, and dense forests. West are grasslands and then the Mississippi River. To the south, **coastal plains** extend to the Atlantic Ocean and the Gulf of Mexico in Florida.

Native Peoples have lived in what is now the southeast of the United States for untold generations, according to oral histories. **Archaeologists** estimate people have lived there for at least 18,000 years. The earliest people hunted, gathered, and fished. People learned to grow corn from far-away trading partners around 900 BC. Local groups then began farming. By approximately 1200 AD, many people were growing corn, beans, and squash. Corn was the base of their diet. It is still a common part of southern American cuisine.

Populations grew. There were four major language groups. The southeast Native Nations also traded with groups from the northeast and the Great Plains.

When Spanish explorers arrived in the 1500s, Native life changed dramatically. The first explorers did not stay long, but they exposed southeastern Native Peoples to new diseases. Many died from smallpox, influenza, and other diseases. Later explorers and settlers brought more problems and changes. Missionaries arrived in the 1600s.

Next came French traders. Later, settlers came from England. Many Native Peoples were killed because of disease or warfare during this time.

Southeastern Native Peoples also started trading more and more with Europeans. This contact caused more changes in society. Groups reorganized. Smaller groups joined with larger bands. They had more power to negotiate with Europeans as a larger group. At the beginning of the 1800s,

Southeastern tribes play stickball, a form of the modern game of lacrosse. In earlier times, it was often used to settle disputes. There were often ceremonies before a match, and players spent days preparing. Stickball is still an important tradition among southeastern Native Peoples. Games begin some ceremonial events and dances. Community teams face off to play for fun, too.

Chickasaw beaded cap, ca. 1800

many of the remaining southeastern Native people were culturally blended. They had adopted new cultural practices that were useful. But they had not completely lost their traditional cultures. Many of them became owners of large farms or plantations. The five major nations were the Cherokee, Chickasaw, Choctaw, Seminole, and the Muscogee (Creek).

However, the flood of white immigrants did not stop demanding more land. Native groups lost land and resources. Tribes tried to negotiate with colonial leaders repeatedly, but the result was always the same. Native Peoples lost their homelands. In the end, the Indian Removal Act of 1830 forced most Native Peoples to relocate. The Seminole Indians fought back with warfare. The Cherokee Nation tried to fight removal with a lawsuit. The Creeks, Choctaw, and Chickasaws also opposed removal. But President Andrew Jackson ordered the U.S. military to make them move. They had to walk to what was called Indian Territory, now the state of Oklahoma. Estimates suggest that approximately 100,000 people were forced from their homeland. Approximately 15,000 died on this march. They faced hunger,

The Indian Removal Act tore Nations apart and caused thousands of deaths.

disease, and exhaustion as they traveled hundreds of miles. This journey has become known as the Trail of Tears.

After removal, the five major nations worked hard to rebuild their economies in Indian Territory. Native groups who managed to stay in their homeland faced racism and harassment. Despite hardships and ongoing challenges, southeastern nations hold on to their traditional cultures in varying ways and to different degrees. Many are reviving their culture and economy.

CHAPTER TWO

CHEROKEE

A 2014 festival celebrated the coming together of the Cherokee Nation and the Eastern Band of Cherokee.

The Cherokee Nation has approximately 300,000 members today. It is one of the largest tribes in the United States. Within the larger group are three federally recognized tribes. They are the Cherokee Nation, the United Keetoowah Band of

Today, apps and computer programs help Cherokee students learn the language.

Cherokee Indians, and the Eastern Band of Cherokee Indians. A federally recognized tribe is considered **sovereign** by the United States government. These tribes establish their own governments and make their own laws. The federal government protects their lands. They also receive services and benefits, such as health care or education.

Cherokee people had a rich culture before European contact. Later, Cherokee culture

An exhibit at the Cherokee Heritage Center remembers the pain of the Trail of Tears.

and society borrowed aspects of European society. Sequoyah is often credited with developing a writing system for the language in the early 1820s. Symbols represent the syllables in the Cherokee language. In 1828, the Cherokee published the first Native

American newspaper, the *Cherokee Phoenix*. It was a **bilingual** newspaper, published in both Cherokee and English.

The U.S. government forced most Cherokees to relocate to Oklahoma on the Trail of Tears. The nation fought the relocation with lawsuits but lost. Today, the Cherokee Nation and the United Keetoowah Band are both based in Tahlequah, Oklahoma. The Eastern Band of Cherokee live in North Carolina in their traditional homeland. The largest of the three groups is the Cherokee Nation. It is a business leader in Oklahoma and runs several successful companies.

The Cherokee National Holiday happens every Labor Day weekend. It is a celebration of Cherokee heritage and one of the largest festivals in Oklahoma. The huge festival includes sports, music, and a parade in downtown Tahlequah. Kids can hear storytellers, practice traditional crafts, and play games.

The stomp dance is a social and religious dance. Many southeastern nations hold stomp dances. It is called "stomp" in English because the dancers make rhythmic steps. Traditionally, rattles give the dance rhythm. The stomp dance is considered a holy event. There are specific rules dancers must follow. For many Cherokee people, this dance is an important part of their cultural heritage.

CHAPTER THREE

CHICKASAW

Chickasaw Princesses ride in the parade at the Red Earth Festival in Oklahoma.

The original homelands of the Chickasaw are present-day Mississippi, Alabama, Tennessee, and Kentucky. In the 1830s, the U.S. government forced the Chickasaw people to relocate to Indian Territory in Oklahoma. They suffered hardships in

The Chickasaw Nation holds a yearly Aviation and Space Academy that gets Chickasaw children excited about science and space.

the journey and rebuilding their lives. But their losses were less than other tribes had experienced because their leaders sold land to pay for them to move. At first they agreed to live with the Choctaw Nation. But in 1856, they separated from the Choctaw. They established their own constitution for their own lands.

Today, the Chickasaw Nation has a strong government that serves the common good of its citizens. The Chickasaw government supports businesses and provides programs and services to its people. In 2000, the tribe began Chickasaw Nation Industries. The business is entirely owned by the Chickasaw Nation. It includes more than a dozen companies. Its services include information technology and work for the oil and gas

The Chickasaw Cultural Center in Oklahoma includes a re-created Chickasaw village.

industry. A portion of its profits supports Chickasaw people in many different ways.

As has happened with Native Nations throughout the continent, speaking the Chickasaw language has declined. During much of the 1900s, many Native children were forced to attend U.S. government-run **residential schools**. They learned English at the schools. They were often punished for speaking their languages or practicing their culture in other ways. Today, there are fewer than 75 Chickasaw speakers. The Nation started a program to bring back the language in 2007. There are language classes, clubs, camps, and a channel for language learning on Chickasaw television. There is even an app called "Chickasaw Language Basics." This was the first language app of its kind developed by a Native Nation.

It is sunny.	Hashi' toomi	(ha-shee too-mee)
It is raining.	Omba	(ohm-ba)
It is cloudy.	Hoshonti	(ho-shon-tee)
It is windy.	Mahli	(ma-lee)
It is snowing.	Oktosha	(owk-too-sha)

SAY IT

CHAPTER FOUR

MUSCOGEE (CREEK)

The original homeland of the Muscogee Nation mostly lay in Alabama, Georgia, and South Carolina. It also included small parts of North Carolina and Florida. The Muscogee are also known as the Creek. Early people constructed impressive

The Muscogee Nation worked with archaeologists from several universities to study and preserve the Etowah Indian Mounds built by their ancestors.

Muscogee men in Oklahoma, 1877, show the tribe's racial mixing, including people with African and European ancestry.

pyramids made of earth along rivers as part of ceremonial complexes. They were a union of several tribes. Towns held their own land and governed themselves.

Many Muscogee had to move to Indian Territory in the 1830s because of the Indian Removal Act. More than 20,000 Muscogee Creeks relocated in 1836 and 1837. In the

A Muscogee leader shows objects kept at Lower Muskogee Creek Tribe headquarters in Georgia.

1890s, the U.S. government passed a law to weaken the Southeast Native Nations. It dissolved their governments. The **reservation** lands were broken up. Individual members owned the land, not the nations themselves. But in recent decades the Muscogee Nation has been rebuilding its government and running its own affairs.

Today, the Muscogee (Creek) Nation is a federally recognized tribe. Its headquarters are in Okmulgee, Oklahoma. It has more than 69,000 members. The nation has its own police force, health center, housing board, and college. There are four other smaller Creek groups in Oklahoma. Other small groups remain in their homelands in the southeast.

Similar to many other Native languages, the Muscogee language is in danger of being lost. A few years ago, Nation members started a language program. Muscogee is now taught in grade school, junior high school, and college.

A few Creek families who provided services to the U.S. government were allowed to stay in Alabama in the 1830s. Today, they are the Poarch Band of Creek Indians. They are the only federally recognized band in Alabama. They have been on their land for more than 150 years. The band has approximately 3,000 members. The band faced decades of discrimination. But it kept its identity and remained a united group. Now the band has casinos, businesses, industry, and farms. It runs the Calvin McGhee Cultural Authority, which oversees cultural education and programs.

The Mvskoke Nation Festival has been held every June in Okmulgee, Oklahoma, for more than 40 years. People come from near and far. They celebrate Muscogee life and heritage. Everyone is welcome. Events include traditional games, arts and crafts, Muscogee hymn singing, a stomp dance, and an all-Native rodeo.

CHAPTER FIVE

CHOCTAW

The ancient homeland of the Choctaw people is Alabama, Mississippi, and Louisiana. The Choctaw were the first of the five major tribes forcibly removed to Indian Territory, starting in 1831. An estimated 15,000 to 20,000 started

Similar to many Nations, the Mississippi Band of Choctaw Indians runs a health care center for its members.

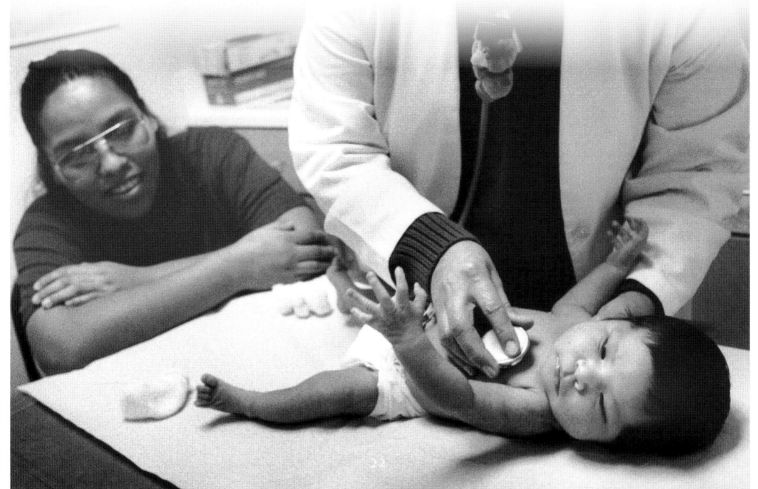

Dancing at the Choctaw Indian Fair, Mississippi

the journey, but many died on the way. Approximately 12,500 survived and reached the new homeland. Some Choctaw were allowed to remain in Mississippi. However, those who stayed were often harassed because of their race. In 1918, the U.S. government set up a reservation for the Choctaw people still in Mississippi. Today, the two major tribes are

Choctaw Casino Resort, Oklahoma

the Choctaw Nation of Oklahoma and the Mississippi Band of Choctaw Indians.

The Choctaw Nation of Oklahoma is the third-largest tribe in the country. It has almost 200,000 members. Once a month, the Nation has a Heritage Day. On this day, members share cultural activities and skills such as language, traditional beading, and pottery with each other. The nation also keeps a record of its artists to recognize and connect with them.

The nation operates seven casinos. Other businesses including manufacturing, a printing company, and several travel plazas.

Choctaw soldiers played a key role in World War I (1914–1918). In 1918, the U.S. military was frustrated because the Germans were capturing much of their communication. By chance, a captain heard two Choctaw soldiers speaking in their own language. He realized the possibility for secret communication. Within hours, they had set up the Choctaw Telephone Squad. They were the first code talkers. The Germans were unable to understand this communication. The code talkers helped the United States win some important battles. However, while Choctaw soldiers were helping U.S. troops, Choctaw children were being taught English in government schools and punished for using their language.

These businesses provide more than 6,000 jobs to nation members, nonmembers, and nonnatives in Oklahoma.

The Mississippi Band of Choctaw Indians makes auto parts and plastics and runs casinos. Its Department of Chahta Immi promotes cultural heritage. Some programs include a language program, a museum, a program to pass down culture, and **archives**. The band also holds workshops to teach traditional Choctaw art, including beadwork, baskets, and clothing.

An earthen mound in Mississippi called Nanih Waiya is the Choctaw people's place of origin in oral histories. Evidence suggests the mound is at least 2,000 years old. Although the Choctaw lost control of this land for almost 200 years, they regained the sacred site in 2006.

SAY IT		
rabbit	chukfi	(chuk-fee)
deer	issi	(is-see)
cat	katos	(ka-tows)
dog	ofi	(oh-fee)
mouse	pinti	(pin-tee)

CHAPTER SIX

SEMINOLE

A Seminole gathering celebrates the life of famous leader Osceola, who lived in the 19th century.

Most Seminole people are descendants of Creek Natives in Florida. In the early 1800s, the population was small, approximately 1,200. With time, Natives escaping removal in other places and blacks fleeing slavery joined the tribe. The population

Seminoles of Florida, 1926

increased to approximately 5,000 by the 1820s.

However, several wars in the next 50 years made the population drop. The U.S. government waged wars against the Seminole people to relocate them to Indian Territory. The three wars were called the Seminole Wars. The Seminole people resisted and

Seminole dolls made from palmetto palm husks wear traditional women's clothing.

their living as hunters, trappers, and guides. Some entertained tourists, wrestling alligators or performing other feats.

By 1913, there were several reservations in Florida. The Seminole Natives of Florida chose to live on reservation land. However, the Miccosukee Tribe of Florida did not. They separated from the Seminole Nation

Seminole people are known for their colorful patchwork clothing. It is a fairly modern tradition. Seminole women developed the patchwork technique in the 1920s. Blocks or bars of alternating colors are sewn into the clothing. The designs can be very complicated. Women started to sell the patchwork items. This became an important source of income. The intricate designs also became a source of cultural pride. Techniques and designs are passed from mothers to daughters.

fought back fiercely. But in the end more than 3,000 people were forced to move to Indian Territory. Only a few hundred managed to remain in Florida. The Seminole in Florida survived on the edges of society. They made

A man in Seminole-style clothing attends a Seminole event.

midcentury. Today, they live on the edge of the Everglades. Both groups operate casinos and other businesses, and the money earned supports programs for members.

The Seminole Nation of Oklahoma has headquarters in Wewoka, Oklahoma. Its members descend from Seminole people who relocated to Indian Territory. The nation has approximately 17,000 members. Each year, it holds a Seminole Nation Days festival, with a powwow, a stomp dance, and traditional clothing contests.

CHAPTER SEVEN

CATAWBA

The Catawba host a multi-tribe powwow on their reservation.

The Catawba Indian Nation is the only federally recognized tribe in South Carolina. Today, the tribe has more than 2,800 enrolled members. The Catawba called themselves *yeh is-WAH h'reh*, which means "people of the river." Their ancestral lands lie along the banks of the Catawba River. The people hunted, farmed, and lived in the Piedmont area of North Carolina.

The Catawba were known as fierce warriors and were often at war with other Native groups. However, they had mostly friendly relationships with European settlers. Unfortunately, the Europeans brought new diseases and many Native Peoples died. The nation came close to dying out more than once. In the 1760s, the king of England granted the Catawba 144,000 acres (58,000 ha) of land because of their friendship. Many other Native groups were forced to relocate in the 1800s. But the Catawba signed a treaty with the state of South Carolina. They were not forced west. However, they had to give up most of their land.

A unique style of pottery is a key part of Catawba heritage. The tradition has been passed down through generations. It has survived war, contact with Europeans, economic and cultural stress, and modern technology like the potter's wheel. The Catawba people have specific methods they use to create their pottery. It is never painted or **glazed**. The simple and elegant pottery is unlike other styles. Over time the number of traditional potters had dropped. Today the tradition has been revived and is being passed on.

Today, the Catawba have a reservation with approximately 800 acres (320 ha) in York County, South Carolina. The nation has many social programs and runs a cultural center. The cultural center offers drumming, dancing, pottery demonstrations, storytelling, and language and history programs.

CHAPTER EIGHT

CHITIMACHA

The 2010 oil spill in the Gulf of Mexico damaged Chitimacha lands and livelihoods. Members testified to claim disaster relief money.

The Chitimacha Tribe of Louisiana is the only tribe in the state that lives on part of its ancient homeland. According to oral history, the Chitimacha have always lived there. Archaeologists have found evidence of people in the area from 6,000 years ago.

The Chitimacha were one of the most powerful Native groups in the Southeast. Then French settlers occupied Louisiana in the early 1700s. They forced many Chitimacha into slavery. In response, a group of Chitimacha killed a white slave owner and others. This led to a 12-year war. Afterward, a treaty established the Chitimacha's land. However, with time, whites took more and more land from the tribe. Today, the tribe owns 963 acres (390 ha). It has 1,300 official members.

The Chitimacha language is unrelated to any other language. The last two speakers of the language were recorded in the 1930s. The language had been **dormant** since then. The tribe's cultural division has used the recordings and other sources to start bringing it back. They even coined words for new concepts, such as *computer* and *bathroom*. Tribe members worked with the Rosetta Stone Endangered Language Program. The language-teaching company works with indigenous groups that have languages with few speakers. Together they created software to teach the language to tribal members anywhere in the world.

computer	qucpamamix	(ooch-pa-ma-mish)
newspaper	nikimti naakxt	(ni-kim-tee-naaksht)
TV	qamwejigi	(am-wed-je-gee)
bathroom	hana ni yupuyna	(ha-nah nee yu-pwe-nah)

SAY IT

CHAPTER NINE

THE TUNICA-BILOXI INDIAN TRIBE OF LOUISIANA

A private collection of modern Tunica crafts

The Tunica-Biloxi Tribes have lived on their reservation in east-central Louisiana for the past two centuries. They were originally two separate tribes who spoke completely different languages. With time, members of the two tribes married each other. This unified the groups as one tribe. Historically, both the Tunica and Biloxi were powerful and successful traders. They formed strong **alliances** with early French settlers.

Today, the tribe has more than 1,200 members. Louisiana officially recognized the tribe in 1976. The tribe fought many

The Tunica Treasure is a collection of tribal **artifacts** that were stolen from ancient graves. After a long lawsuit, the collection was eventually returned to the Tunica-Biloxi Tribe. This was very important to the tribe. The lawsuit also laid the foundation for a federal law. In 1990, Congress passed the Native American Graves Protection and Repatriation Act. This law concerns cultural items such as remains or sacred objects held by museums or state or federal agencies. Items that can be identified with a tribe must be returned to the tribe. The collection is now in the Tunica-Biloxi Cultural and Educational Resources Center.

legal battles to gain federal recognition. They received it in 1981. As was common on reservations throughout the early 1900s, residents of the Tunica-Biloxi reservation once lived in shacks with no running water. The tribe used benefits from federal recognition to improve housing for tribal members.

In 1994, the tribe opened the Paragon Casino Resort on its reservation. With more than 1,780 employees, it is the largest private employer in the area. This has strengthened their economy. Income from the business allows the tribe to provide services and facilities to members. The tribe also donates money to nonprofit organizations.

The motto on the Tunica-Biloxi's flag is "Cherishing Our Past, Building for Our Future." The tribe has held onto its cultural

H~hch,
uhk'oniseman
rɔhpanrikin'ataneni.
Now his people were
coming too close.
H~hch, hichut'una
amayisahkun,
nar'unihkeni.
So, the two eagles
flew in opposite
directions.

identity for centuries. It continues to pass on its heritage. It holds the Tunica-Biloxi Pow Wow. The event brings members together to celebrate culture and traditions. Camps teach children about their language and traditions. In 2011, the tribe opened the Tunica-Biloxi Cultural and Educational Resources Center. The museum teaches people from outside the community about the Tunica-Biloxi and protects the tribe's heritage.

Brenda Lintinger wrote a children's book in her Tunica ancestors' language to help revive it.

alliances (uh-LYE-uhn-siz) Alliances are agreements to work together for some result. The Tunica-Biloxi made alliances with French settlers.

archaeologists (ahr-kee-OL-uh-jists) Archaeologists are people who study people and cultures from long ago. Archaeologists work with Native Peoples to understand ancient artifacts.

archives (AHR-kives) Archives are collections of related documents or other things that are stored in a library or other public place. Some tribes keep archives in their cultural centers.

artifacts (AHR-tuh-fakts) Artifacts are objects made or changed by humans from the past. Ancient artifacts give information about how early Natives lived.

bilingual (bye-LING-gwuhl) A person who is bilingual is able to speak two languages well. Many Native Americans are bilingual.

coastal plains (KOHST-ul playns) Coastal plains are areas of flat, low land near the coast of the sea or ocean. There are coastal plains near the Atlantic Ocean.

dormant (DOR-muhnt) A dormant language is one that is not being used. The Chitimacha language was dormant until tribal members started working to bring it back into use.

glazed (GLAYZD) Pottery that is glazed has a thin coat of liquid applied before it is fired to give it a shiny, colorful finish. Pottery made by Catawba potters is never glazed.

reservation (rez-er-VAY-shuhn) A reservation is an area of land set aside for Native use. A reservation is run by its own government and provides services to its residents.

residential schools (rez-i-DEN-shuhl SKOOLS) Residential schools were boarding schools for Native children funded by the Canadian or U.S. federal governments. Until the middle of the 20th century, many Native children were forced to go to residential schools.

sovereign (SAHV-ruhn) Something that is sovereign is independent. Native nations recognized by the government are sovereign and can control their own affairs.

TO LEARN MORE

BOOKS

Benoit, Peter. *The Trail of Tears*. New York: Children's Press, 2012.

King, David C. *First People: An Illustrated History of American Indians*. New York: DK Publishing, 2008.

Rumford, James. *Sequoyah: The Cherokee Man Who Gave His People Writing*. Boston: Houghton Mifflin, 2004.

WEB SITES

Visit our Web site for links about Native Nations of the Southeast:

childsworld.com/links

Note to Parents, Teachers, and Librarians: We routinely verify our Web links to make sure they are safe and active sites. So encourage your readers to check them out!